SHOWING THE WAY

A Guidebook for Lent

KATHRYN TURNER

A Wellspring Resource
SHOWING THE WAY A Guidebook for Lent

MCCRIMMONS
Great Wakering, Essex

First published in Great Britain in 1999 by
McCrimmon Publishing Co. Ltd.
10-12 High Street, Great Wakering, Essex SS3 0EQ
Telephone 01702-218956 Fax 01702-216082
Email: mccrimmons@dial.pipex.com

ISBN 0 85597 603 9 (Showing the Way - A Guidebook for Lent)
ISBN 0 85597 604 7 (Showing the Way - Leader's Book)

Page illustrations - The Benedictine Nuns of Turvey Abbey
Cover and page design: Jim Dansie, Great Wakering, Essex

Typeset in Garramond Book 11/12pt
Printed by Antony Rowe Ltd.

A/II

CONTENTS

SHOWING THE WAY

A Guidebook for Lent

INTRODUCTION

Prayer is an exercise. It takes practice and, just to cheer you up, takes a lifetime to perfect.
It brings with it times of great insight and joy
and times of utter boredom and irritation.

The Reflections in "Showing the Way" are based on the Readings used each day at the Weekday Masses. Each week has been put under the umbrella of the Sunday Gospel and a theme related to it.
They can be used on your own or in a group. If you are on your own, you can read the Main Gospel at the beginning and at the end of the week - and see how your week's reflections have deepened your understanding of it.
If you are in a group, that will happen, hopefully, during the Meetings.
The Scripture references for each day are given so that you can read the whole reading if you have time.
You can jot down thoughts as they come in your prayer-time -
or summarise them at the end.
This is well-worth doing.
Even over the course of Lent, you will be amazed by how much you receive and how much you could have lost without recording it.

Setting the scene for your prayer - a few practicalities

It is helpful to build up a habit of prayer. Somehow, going to the same place at around the same time and having the same settling-down routine, all help to make prayer easier.
When you pray, choose a time and a place where you will not be disturbed.
Take the 'phone off the hook, if necessary.
Make sure that you are warm and comfortable (only books about saints say that discomfort is a good thing for prayer!)
Try different postures for Prayer - sitting, standing, kneeling, lying-flat on your back (risky if you pray last thing at night!)

Create a prayer-area

Invest in a candle - and incense-sticks if they appeal to you.
Find a picture that appeals to you.
It could be a religious picture - or a picture of a flower, a view, an open door - anything that helps you. If you can, leave your prayer-area set up. It will help to remind you of your Prayer - even when you don't have time to pray!

Getting started

It can be very helpful to read the Readings (or at least the extract for the day) - and prompts for reflection - in advance.
If your Prayer-time is in the morning, read the day's Readings the night before.
If your Prayer-time is in the evenings, look at them in the morning.
A lot of Prayer goes on deep-down, and a bit of advance preparation gets things moving.

Time to pray...

After lighting your candle etc. focus your thoughts on what you are there for.
You might just gaze at the candle or your picture.
Some people spend a few moments becoming aware of their breathing, others find music helps.
Others use a mantra to help to still the mind.
In keeping with our Lenten theme, you may like to try this verse from Psalm 25:

Breathe in slowly and say (silently!) *Lord, make me know Your ways.*
Breathe out slowly and say (silently!) *Lord, teach me Your paths*

When you are ready, read the Readings in full - and pause for a few moments (maybe going back to your breathing or mantra).
Then , read the extract and the prompts for reflection and give yourself time to explore the thoughts and ideas that come.
How long you spend depends on the time you have - but, if you can, allow 15 minutes or so for this. It can take a while to settle deeply into the Prayer.

(Note: It is probably at this point that you will remember that the car needs petrol, the kitchen floor needs washing or the cat needs putting out. These are called "Distractions". You may never give a thought to these things at any other time, but the minute you start praying, they appear with an insistence that can take your breath away.
How you deal with your distractions will depend on what they are but, in general, they are rarely things that have to be done there and then... (though the cat may be an exception!).
Do not allow them to become a battleground - that is giving them more importance than they deserve.
Acknowledge them - promise yourself that you will tackle the jobs when the Prayer-time is over or at a more convenient time - and then firmly but gently turn your mind back to your music, your mantra - or whatever you find helps you to re-focus.

Console yourself also with two thoughts:

- *The greatest pray-ers in history were also plagued by distractions (Teresa of Avila was quite open about this)*
- *If you have 50 distractions and each time make a conscious effort to turn back to the Prayer in hand, then that is 50 little prayers.*
  You may end up feeling that you have wasted the time - but you haven't. God values the little turnings-back as much as the epic raptures of His more accomplished saints.)

This may be the time to jot thoughts down -or it can wait until the end.

How the prayer will feel

How prayer feels depends partly on you but even more on what God is doing.
It may feel as if you are thinking about the questions.
It may lead you into an imaginative prayer where you enter the story - or discover images and insights that seem to come from no-where.
It may be that you become so deeply involved in the Prayer that you are unaware of anything happening at all.
It may be totally dry and boring.

Do not judge your Prayer by how it feels.
Quite often, it will only be later on that you see what your Prayer has been about - as images and ideas re-appear and new links are made between them.
If your Prayer feels particularly dry, it might be helpful to chat to someone who understands Prayer. It may well be that God is working something through deep within you - below the level of consciousness.
Try to persevere - it will get better.
In the meantime, try to remember that you are giving this time to God to do what He wants - even if that means that you don't get the spiritual fireworks that others seem to get.
God treasures your faithfulness to Prayer - especially when it is hard-going for you.

The closing thoughts

The closing thoughts are there to help you draw your prayer together - a time to talk to Jesus as a friend and companion about your prayer and what it might mean for your life.
If your prayer has been deep and powerful, they can help you to make the transition back to the "real" world.
Do not hurry them.

Sharing the prayer – in a group

"Sharing your prayer" is not meant to be a soul-baring exercise.
Sharing something of your prayer helps you to get more out of it.
You also help others - and can be helped by them -
as you see things that seem to be coincidence -
and which are signs of the Holy Spirit working among you.

You may decide to join a group who are following the "Showing the Way" booklet through Lent.
Here, you will have a chance to see how your daily prayer and reflections relate to some of the main Lent Gospels.
If you are choosing this option, you will find that you don't cover all the Week's readings before your Meeting. This need not be a problem as your shared prayer and discussion should help you to get more from the Readings and reflections that remain.

Sharing the prayer – with a companion

It is a strong prayer-tradition to have a prayer-companion
Such a person is sometimes, and not very accurately, called a "Spiritual Director".
Celtic Christians used the term "anam chara" which means "soul-friend" .

You may already be blessed with such a companion on your spiritual journey - or feel that this is something you could try. It can be beneficial to meet regularly with someone you trust to share the fruits - or boredom! - of your prayer.

It can be a real joy to share the "good bits" -
and a source of real encouragement to carry on when the going gets a bit tougher!

A little aside

It may be that something comes up in the Prayer that leaves you uncomfortable or unhappy.
Please note - everything that comes up in Prayer comes onto Holy Ground.
You are not alone - but are in a praying parish community, supported by their prayer.
You may well find that, over the days and weeks, you will find yourself able to move on from the things causing you pain and discomfort - and experience for yourself the power of God's healing love for you.
If it feels too hard to cope with - you might take it to the Sacrament of Reconciliation - or talk to a trusted friend or companion.
You can also ask for a confidential meeting with a priest, minister or spiritual director in which to work out what is happening - and how best to work with what God is doing in and for you.

Above all else - see this as a time of grace.
A time to learn to know yourself and God a little better.

Fresh-Air Prayer

Each week, there is a suggestion for a Prayer to be done outside.
It is offered for Saturday, but can be used on any day that is convenient.
Although it may feel strange, this kind of Prayer is often part of a Retreat Experience.
Somehow, being outside opens the Prayer up.
Try it!

Psalm numbering

You will see that, on most days, two Psalm numbers are offered. This is not to give you a choice - but trying to work with one of the little problems that arise from time-to-time in different versions of the Bible. Some of the Psalms are numbered differently in different Bibles - depending on whether that version treats Psalm 9 as one long psalm (Greek numbering) or two shorter ones (Hebrew numbering). The problem resolves itself at Psalm no. 147 but it is enough to cause some confusion!
To see which number you should use, find "The Lord is my shepherd..." in your Bible. It will be either Psalm 22 or 23. If it is number 22, use the first number given each day; if it is 23, use the second.
Easy, isn't it!

and finally –

No one can predict what will happen over the next few weeks - what joys and new discoveries.
Treat it as a special time of grace - a time to learn to know yourself and God a little better.

Week before Lent – Setting Out

THURSDAY AFTER ASH WEDNESDAY

Prepare for Prayer - See the suggestions above.
If you have a way of prayer that works for you, it is probably easier to stick with that.
If you are working up to that, you will probably find it helpful to try out various possibilities and find the way that suits you best.

Scripture: Deuteronomy 30: 15-20; Psalm 1; Luke 9: 22-25

Jesus said, "If anyone wants to be a follower of mine, let them take up their cross and follow me."

Spend a few minutes reading and then reflecting on this.
Then, if they help, use the questions to focus your thoughts.

Did you ever consciously decide to follow Jesus? Or did it "just happen"?
If you did make a decision, when and how did you make it?
What do you hope following Jesus will mean for you this Lent?
What cross might He ask you to bear?

In your own words, tell Jesus that you want to follow Him more closely this Lent. Ask Him to help you to bear any cross that comes your way over the next few weeks.

FRIDAY AFTER ASH WEDNESDAY

Prepare for Prayer

Scripture: Isaiah 58: 1-9; Psalm 50(51); Matthew 9: 14-15

Jesus said, "The time will come for the bridegroom to be taken away from them, and then they will fast."

Read and reflect on this for a few minutes.

Have you ever fasted? How did it feel - while you were fasting and afterwards?
Friday was for many years a day when Catholics did not eat meat - as a reminder of the great Friday when the Bridegroom was taken away from us.

In your own words, express your sorrow for the times you have sinned.
Thank Him for His love for you in spite of this.
Offer a small sacrifice - to fast, not eat a favoured food, or some other gift of your choosing as a sign of your love and gratitude for His great love.
Ask for His help in perseverance.

SATURDAY AFTER ASH WEDNESDAY

Prepare for Prayer

Scripture: Isaiah 58: 9-14; Psalm 85(86); Luke 5: 27-32

Jesus said, "I have not come to call the virtuous, but sinners to repentance."

Read and reflect on this for a few minutes.

If you are well, you don't need a doctor.
If you are already perfect, you have no need of Jesus.
Why do you need Jesus?

In your own words, thank Jesus for the things He loves about you.
Ask Him to show the things He wants you to change.
Give Him time to answer!

This time of year bears little resemblance to a desert - but it can be ju
Go into the countryside - or find a spot in a town to sit and watch wh
happening.
Reflect on the following thoughts:
What do people mean when they say we live in a "spiritual desert" these days?
What is missing from people's lives?

What do people do to try and fill the emptiness inside themselves?
Do these things make them happy?

Think about yourself - and about how the bleakness of what you see around you reflects the bleak places inside yourself.
What do you long for?
What do *you* do to try to fill the emptiness?

Like Jesus, we sometimes have to go to bleak and empty places to see ourselves clearly and to get things into proportion.
As you begin Lent, what do you see in yourself - the good as well as the bad?
Is there a particular emptiness or longing that you need to look at this year?
Recognising the "emptiness" for what it is is the first step.
This is the space in you that only God can fill and bring to life.

Look at the world as you see it today - and then, imagine it changing as the weather gets warmer and the sun becomes stronger.
Try to look at your own emptiness - and imagine that changing as you go through Lent - as your prayer gets stronger and your soul responds to the warmth of God's love.

It won't happen all at once - and probably not in the way you expect - but it will happen.

In your own words, tell Jesus about this emptiness inside you and ask for His help during Lent.
Ask Him for strength - courage - perseverance - whatever you think you are going to need to help you.
Above all, ask Him to remind you of His constant love for you.

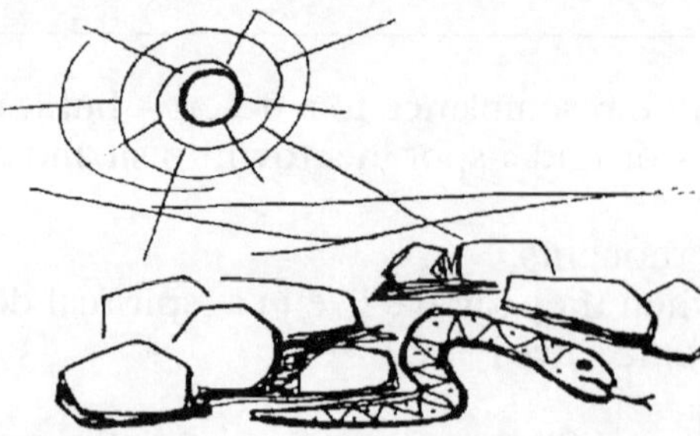

First week of Lent
GATHERING FOR THE JOURNEY

Year A - The Temptation of Jesus (Matthew 4: 1-11)
Year B - The Temptation of Jesus (Mark 1: 12-15)
Year C - The Temptation of Jesus (Luke 4: 1-13)

MONDAY

Prepare for Prayer

Scripture: Leviticus 19:1-2, 11-18; Psalm 18(19); Matthew 25: 31-46

Jesus said, "In so far as you fed, or clothed or visited the least of My brothers and sisters, you did it to Me."

Think about your everyday life and the things that you do for others.
What other "good works" could you add to the list?
What are the things that you avoid - or try not to notice?

In your own words, thank Jesus for the good things that you do.
Ask Him to increase your awareness of doing them for Him.
Ask Him also to open your eyes to the things you'd rather not see or act on.

TUESDAY

Prepare for Prayer

Scripture: Isaiah 55: 10-11; Psalm 33(34); Matthew 6: 7-15

Jesus said, "In your prayers do not babble – your Father knows what you need before You ask Him"

What messages of love have you given to - or received from - a child?
What were they like - long and complicated? - or simple and loving?
Hopefully, you get the right answer - and see that as the way Jesus taught us to pray!

Imagine Jesus leading you in saying the Our Father - as you would lead a child - "say after Me..."
How does the prayer feel?

WEDNESDAY

Prepare for Prayer

Scripture: Jonah 3: 1-10; Psalm 50(51); Luke 11: 29-32

The crowds got even bigger and Jesus addressed them. "This is a wicked generation; it is asking for a sign."

The crowds were following Jesus because He was a novelty.
Who attracts the great crowds in our generation?
What sign would convince our generation of the love and power of Jesus?

If you have been blessed with a sign of God's love for you, now is a good time to be thankful for it.
If you have been too keen on seeing signs and wonders as fuel for your Faith, maybe this is a good day to apologise.

THURSDAY

Prepare for Prayer

Scripture: Esther 4: 17 l-z (Jerusalem Bible) 14: 3-5; 12-14 (NRSV Catholic Edition)* 14: 3-5; 12-14 (King James/Authorised Version)*; Psalm 137(138); Matthew 7: 7-12*

Jesus said, "Ask and you will receive; search and you will find; knock and the door will be opened to you."

When have you had to persevere in prayer?
How was the prayer answered? Was it dramatic and miraculous? Or did it seem like an everyday coincidence?
What are you asking - or searching for at the moment?

In your own words, remind Jesus of His promise.
Ask for patience - or strength as you wait for the answer or great find.

---

* This part of the Book of Esther is not found in all Bibles - and, as you can see, is not always easy to find when it is! The Book of Esther has two versions - a Hebrew one and a Greek one. This extract is from the Greek version and is referred to as deutero-canonical or apocryphal. It is a Song - or Prayer - that Esther prayed in her anguish and despair. If you don't have it - read through Ch. 4 to get an idea of what was happening around Esther - and then read, as her Song, Psalm 130.

FRIDAY

Prepare for Prayer

Scripture: Ezekiel 18: 21-28; Psalm 129(130); Matthew 5: 20-26

Jesus said, "If you are bringing your offering to the altar and there remember that your brother or sister has something against you, leave your offering there before the altar, go and be reconciled with your brother or sister first, and then come back and present your offering."

Is there someone you need to be reconciled with?
A day of fasting or abstaining is a good one on which to pray for the strength and courage to make the first move in being reconciled.
It is also a good one on which to pray for the love and courage to forgive.

In your own words, tell Jesus about people you have hurt - or been hurt by.
Show Him where you are stuck in the human emotions of pain and anger - and ask Him to transform them into love and a desire to forgive and to seek forgiveness.
Ask Him to help you to put things right.

SATURDAY

Prepare for Prayer

Scripture: Deuteronomy 26: 16-19; Psalm 118(119)
(suggest verses 1-8 - rather than the whole of it…); Matthew 5: 43-48

Jesus said, "Love your enemies and pray for those who persecute you."

Anybody who says being a Christian is for softies hasn't really considered the strength it takes to do what Jesus is telling us here!
Who is your enemy?
Who is persecuting you - or at least giving you a hard time?

Tell Jesus about the problem - and about how hard this teaching is in "real-life"
Try a prayer of imagination…
Be still and relaxed and imagine that you are breathing in a coloured light.
When the light has filled you, have a practice by thinking of someone you really like, and let the light flow into them.
Now try the same thing with someone who is giving you a hard time.
If at first you don't succeed…

FRESH-AIR PRAYER

Take yourself off for an hour or so for a walk - somewhere where you feel you can really breathe!
If you have a prayer companion, he or she could go too.

Begin the walk by mentally and spiritually preparing for prayer - candles are probably not an option (this time!)
Imagine Jesus as a companion as you walk.

If you have had problems with the Prayer Exercises this week, tell Jesus and/or your companion about them. (N.B. - good prayer companions can also share silences!)

Find a spot to stop.

This can be a view, near a tree, looking at the sea or a river - whatever helps you in the next bit.
Spend a few minutes really looking and listening - get to know what you are looking at.

Now, imagine the scene as it would have been 25/50/100/! years ago (before you were born) - when the tree was small, the plants not grown so tall, when people wearing different clothes might have stood where you are now
See Jesus there - just as at home with them as is He is now with you.

Now, imagine the scene in 25/50/100/!years time (after you have died) - what will be different?
Again, imagine Jesus equally at home there.

If you are very imaginative, you can go back to dinosaurs and forward to sci-fi stuff!
And always, Jesus is at home there.

Allow yourself time to play and pray with the ideas.
What do you learn?
What becomes of your problems?

Second Week of Lent

THE EVERYDAY TOUCHED BY THE DIVINE

Year A - The Transfiguration (Matthew 17: 1-9)
Year B - The Transfiguration (Mark 9: 2-10)
Year C - The Transfiguration (Luke 9: 28-36)

MONDAY

Scripture: Daniel 9: 4-10; Psalm 78(79); Luke 6: 36-38

Jesus said, "Give and there will be gifts for you: a full measure, pressed down, shaken together, and running over, will be poured into your lap; because the amount you measure out is the amount you will be given back."

Do a little experiment.
Put flour into a jar until it is full.
Now shake the flour down, press it down and see how much more flour you can fit in.
Repeat until the jar is overflowing!

In your own words, tell Jesus about your experiment.
What have you learnt about God's love for you?
What have you learnt about the love asked of you - for God and your neighbour?
You may want to keep your jar as a reminder!

TUESDAY

Scripture Isaiah 1: 10, 16-20; Psalm 49(50); Matthew 23: 1-12

Jesus said, "Anyone who exalts himself will be humbled and anyone who humbles himself will be exalted."

Everyone likes to be noticed - especially for something good.
What is the difference between being noticed and appreciated - and making sure everyone knows that you are "God's gift" to something?
Being humble is not being a doormat - you are allowed to be praised and appreciated for the good you do! - So what have you done that is praise-worthy?

Being humble is seeing yourself in proportion - there will always be people "better" than you - so who?
And sometimes, we can think we are "being humble" but only so that everyone notices - have you ever done this?

In your own words, tell Jesus about the problem of true humility.
Ask Him to show you where your goodness comes from.
Show your appreciation and praise for the One who is the generous Source of all life and goodness.

WEDNESDAY

Scripture: Jeremiah 18: 18-20; Psalm 30(31); Matthew 20: 17-28

Jesus said, "Anyone who wants to be great among you must be your servant. The Son of Man came not to be served but to serve."

Who would you say is a good example of this teaching?
Do they seem demeaned by their service?
Does their generosity of spirit make them puffed-up?
How does this teaching relate to yesterday's thoughts?

Thank God for the example of those who serve - and who are made great by their service.
Ask Jesus to help you follow that example - and maybe offer a few pointers as to where you need to improve.

THURSDAY

Scripture: Jeremiah 17: 5-10; Psalm 1; Luke 16: 19-31

Jesus said, "The rich man used to feast magnificently every day. Lazarus longed to fill himself with the scraps that fell from the rich man's table."

The rich man has benefited much from the good things in life. At the time when Jesus told this story, wealth was a sign of God's favour - and poverty a sign of God's displeasure.
Jesus turns this upside-down when He shows the rich man in hell and Lazarus in heaven…
It becomes a question of the rich man's response to the generosity he has received from God - should he really take it as pat-on-the-back from God? or a cue to find people with whom he can be equally generous?
Which did he choose?

Be honest now… which of the two situations has God placed you in?
What did you do to deserve such generosity?
And what is your response to it?

In your prayer, today, think about the good things that you have - and express your thanks at being so generously provided for.
Now, contrast that with what other people have - how might you be being asked to share God's generosity with them?

Ask Jesus to show you ways in which you can act as generously as God. Come up with specific things to do - and promise to do them

FRIDAY

Scripture: Genesis 37: 3-4, 12-13, 17-28; Psalm 104(105); Matthew 21: 33-43, 45-46

Jesus said, "The Kingdom of God will be taken away from you and given to a people who will produce its fruit."

The Kingdom is about bearing fruits - of kindness, compassion, justice, integrity and many more.
It is a great gift but comes with a responsibility - to use it or lose it.
How does your life bear the fruits of the Kingdom?
What aspects of your life encourage you to be fruitful?
Where are you less fruitful?

Talk to Jesus about your desire to be fruitful.
Ask Him about the areas where you find it hard to be fruitful. What needs to change?

SATURDAY

Scripture: Micah 7: 14-15, 18-29; Psalm 102(103); Luke 15: 1-3, 11-32

Try to read the whole Gospel and see where your attention is held.

When have you been the Younger Son?
When have you been the Elder Son?
When have you been the Father?
Notice we do not say "like" the Sons and the Father. Scripture works best if you can really enter the story as you. This is a good story to put this kind of prayer into practice.

Using the story of the Prodigal Son.
Spend a while reflecting on the gifts you have received from God - your talents, the people you love etc.
In the fresh-air, look again at the list you have made.
Reflect on the ways in which you have squandered or spoilt the gifts that you have received.
Note them down.
This is a tough exercise but very valuable.
You may well want to bring your reflections to a private Act of Reconciliation - or speak of them with a trusted companion. Remember that nothing is unforgivable if sorrow is genuine.

If someone you love does this exercise, treat them gently on their return.
Don't pry - just love.

Third week of Lent

THE CHALLENGE OF GOD

Year A - The Woman at the Well (John 4: 5-42)
Year B - The Clearing of the Temple (John 2:13-25)
Year C - The Parable of the Fig Tree (Luke 13: 1-9)

MONDAY

Scripture: 2 Kings 5: 1-15; Psalm 41(42); Luke 4: 24-30

Jesus said, "No prophet is ever accepted in his own country."

Discipleship costs.
Speaking the Truth does not always make us popular.
Like Jesus, we can find that those closest to us are the most critical of our beliefs.
When have you found this to be true?
When have found love and acceptance "outside"?

In your own words, talk to Jesus about the times when you have been hurt or ridiculed for your belief in Him. Allow Him to share the pain - especially where the conflict has been with those closest to you.
Ask Him to increase your strength and stamina in speaking about the things you know to be true.

TUESDAY

Scripture: Daniel 3: 25, 34-43; Psalm 24(25); Matthew 18: 21-35

Jesus said, "The king said, 'I cancelled all that debt of yours when you appealed to me. Were you not bound, then, to have pity on your fellow servant just as I had pity on you?' "

Jesus often puts two people into His stories - one who lives as God wants, the other who doesn't - so, which is which here!
One lives from the inside out - his inner compassion leads him to act - forgiving the debt of his servant.
What comes from the other is selfishness and spite and a refusal to forgive.
Remember with gratitude all the debts and sins of yours that have been cancelled.

Feel the freedom that comes with God's forgiveness.
Are there any wrongs or debts that someone has against you?

In your own words, thank God for His great mercy in forgiving you so abundantly.
Ask Jesus' opinion - and help - in dealing with any of the debts or wrongs that you feel upset about.
Give Him time to answer.

WEDNESDAY

Scripture: Deuteronomy 4: 1,5-9; Psalm 147(148); Matthew 5: 17-19

Jesus said, "The one who keeps the commandments and teaches others to do the same will be considered great in the Kingdom of heaven."

Do you know the Ten Commandments?
How did Jesus summarise them?
Jesus also said that it is by our love for one another that people will know that we are His friends.

A popular phrase in the Church is "teaching by example"
Jesus is not just singling out teachers and parents and catechists here to teach.
All His disciples share this ministry.
How does your example teach people about the love of God and the wisdom of His rules for life - even if they are not the easiest rules to keep!
Have you ever seen the good effect that your living of your faith has had on others?

As always, in your own words, speak to Jesus as you would to a friend.
Ask Him to show you where you have helped others by your example.
How has your love for someone shown that you are a friend of Jesus?
Ask Him to point out where you could improve.

THURSDAY

Scripture: Jeremiah 7: 23-28; Psalm 94(95); Luke 11: 14-23

Jesus said, "He who is not with me is against Me; and he who does not gather with Me scatters."

Jesus depends on us to continue His work.
How do you work with Jesus?
What - or who - do you help to gather into His kingdom?
Where do you find refreshment when the work gets hard-going?

You may wish to tell Jesus, today, that you do want to work with Him in building up His kingdom.
Ask Him to show you how you can do this in the ordinary things that you do.
Ask for His constant refreshment when things become hard and dry for you.

FRIDAY

Scripture: Hosea 14: 2-10; Psalm 80(81); Mark 12: 28-34

Jesus said, "You must love the Lord your God with all your heart, with all your soul, with all your mind, and with all your strength. You must love your neighbour as yourself."

This takes us back to Wednesday's Gospel - and reminds us of where our obedience to the commandments comes from. It should not be fear or mindless obedience - but flow from a love of God deep inside us.
Do you love God with all your heart and soul and mind and strength? - or are you a bit afraid to?
Do you love yourself? You are a unique creation of God - do you love and cherish the little bit of God's great creation that is you?
Do you recognise your neighbour as another unique creation of God? Do you love and cherish them?

Talk to Jesus about these commandments.
Reflect on ways in which you can polish up your love and service.
Does someone you know need a listening ear or a helping hand? Could they be yours?

SATURDAY

Scripture: Exodus 17: 1-7; Psalm 94(95); John 4: 5-42

(Alternative readings for 3rd Week in Lent)

Jesus said, "Anyone who drinks this water will get thirsty again; but anyone who drinks the water that I shall give will never be thirsty again: the water that I shall give will turn into a spring inside him, welling up to eternal life."

A long but important Gospel.
Try a Prayer of imagination.
Read the Gospel
Take it slowly and give your soul and Jesus time to work together!
Build up a picture of a dry, barren desert landscape.
Picture yourself at the side of a well. You are hot and tired and thirsty.
Someone offers you a drink - maybe the Samaritan woman.
You sit and listen to the conversation between her and Jesus.
(Don't read it - just let bits float up into your imagination)
Imagine Jesus turning to you and asking what you are thirsty for.
What do you answer?
How does Jesus respond?
End your prayer - hopefully, feeling thankful for what you have received.

A little practical exercise

Make a record of how much water you use in a day.
Reflect on your need of water.
Reflect on what this teaches you about this Gospel and your need of Jesus.

Water is essential for today's Prayer.
Go to the sea, a lake, a pond, a river.
Spend time just gazing and listening.
Make a note - written or mental - of all that you see or hear.

Think about all the life the water supports - in the water and around its edges.
What do they tell you about God's love for the world? And God's love for you?

Think about the power of water - as it slowly washes away banks or dramatically breaks down cliffs.
What could this tell you about your spiritual life?
Are there parts of you that God is working on slowly and patiently - bringing about gentle change?
What experiences have you had where God has shattered illusions - or turned your world upside-down?

If you can, try to go without drinking for a while - just enough to make you thirsty.
Savour the cool, clear water that quenches your thirst.
Thank God for the gift of water.
Thank Jesus for being the living-spring that quenches our deepest thirsts.

Fourth Week of Lent

THE GOD WHO OPENS OUR EYES TO LOVE

Year A - The Healing of the Blind Man (John 9: 1-41)
Year B - God loved the world so much... (John 3: 14-21)
Year C - The Prodigal Son (Luke 15: 1-3, 11-32)

MONDAY

Scripture: Isaiah 65: 17-21; Psalm 29(30); John 4: 43-54

Jesus said, "Go home, your son will live." The man believed what Jesus had said and started on his way; and while he was still on the journey back his servants met him with the news that his son was alive.

What does this man see in Jesus?
When have you prayed for a sign or wonder?
Has your faith been shaken by God's "failure" to answer your prayer dramatically?
When have you had the experience of deciding just to "carry on with life" - only to see that God has answered your prayer in a way you hadn't expected?

In your own words, talk to Jesus about the desire for signs and miracles.
Ask Him for the faith to "carry on with life" and to trust that, as you do, He is answering your prayers.

TUESDAY

Scripture: Ezekiel 47: 1-9,12; Psalm 45(46); John 5: 1-3, 5-16

Jesus said, "Do you want to be well again?"

This seems a strange question to ask anyone - let alone someone who has been ill for 38 years.
What do you think the man thought of Jesus?
There is, though, some truth in Jesus' question.
We get used to our crutches, to our weaknesses. They can provide a useful excuse for not doing things we don't want to, or for not taking full responsibility for our lives.

Our crutches can be less obvious too - they could be things that keep us busy and stop us living life to the full.
What are your crutches or convenient weaknesses?

In your own words, tell Jesus about the things you have recognised as stopping you from living life to the full.
Ask Him for the courage to be made well and to face the challenges that may lie ahead.
Ask for help in facing the world as "someone different".

WEDNESDAY

Scripture: Isaiah 49: 8-15; Psalm 144(145); John 5: 17-30

Jesus said, "Whoever listens to My words and believes in the One who sent Me, has eternal life."

Jesus does not say that those who listen and believe *will* have eternal life, He says that they have it.
We tend to think that eternal life starts after death, but this is not altogether accurate.
We have been baptised into the death and resurrection of Jesus.
We share His Risen Life.
Within us are the seeds of eternal life - even if we cannot always see them.
Our life-after-death will only prove what our life-before-death was about.
This will be the moment of truth when, as St Paul puts it, our hidden self has grown stronger in knowledge and love of God and we know the infinite love that Jesus has for us - and, at last, can experience it to the full.
When and how have you felt the love of God, your Creator and the Son, your Saviour?
When have you felt the power of the Spirit?

Speak to Jesus of your fear of death.
Ask Him to help you to see the seeds of eternal life within you - the beauty you have experienced, the love you have known and shown etc.

THURSDAY

Scripture: Exodus 32: 7-14; Psalm 105(106); John 5: 31-47

Jesus said, "How can you believe, since you look to one another approval and are not concerned with the approval that comes from the one God?"

Even with knowledge of the love of God and of Jesus and the power of the Spirit, we still lack confidence in ourselves.
Even though we know that we have God's approval for the good things we do and say, we still need approval from other people.
In moderation, that is no bad thing - especially if it confirms our determination to live the Christian life to the full.
Sometimes, though, we give more weight to the approval of others than we do to God's.

When have you chosen the approval of your family, friends, colleagues etc. in preference to God's?

In your own words, express sorrow for letting other people's opinions of you matter more than God's.
Pray for the wisdom to see the difference between life-giving approval - which will always be in tune with God's - and deadening approval - which keeps you bound to "what will people think of me?"

FRIDAY

Scripture: Wisdom 2: 1, 12-22; Psalm 33(34); John 7: 1-2, 10, 25-30

Jesus said, "Yes, you know Me and you know where I came from. Yet I have not come of Myself: no, there is One who sent Me and I really come from Him."

The people of Jesus' time knew He came from Nazareth. This was a stumbling-block to people who expected the Christ to appear from nowhere. They saw Jesus as a local carpenter who had lived among them for 30-odd years.
How do you see Jesus?
Do you believe that Jesus was sent by God?

In your own words, tell Jesus of your faith in Him as the Christ, the One who has come into the world to save it.

SATURDAY

Scripture: Micah 7: 7-9; Psalm 26(27); John 9: 1-41
(Alternative Readings given for 4th Week of lent)

The man who had been blind said, "Now here is an astonishing thing! Ever since the world began it is unheard of for anyone to open the eyes of a man who was born blind; if this man were not from God, he couldn't do such a thing." "Are you trying to teach us," they replied, "and you a sinner through and through, since you were born!" And they drove him away.

We have the contrast between the blind man who sees and those with sight who don't.
There is physical sight and there is spiritual sight.
Give thanks today for your physical sight.
Make a note of the things that you would most miss if the gift of sight was lost.
Try to cherish them particularly today.
We are also trying to develop the gift of spiritual sight - the habit of looking for God in all things.
As you live the day, try to spot God - in the good things you see, hear, touch, taste and smell; in the acts of love; in the gestures of kindness.
At the end of the day, give thanks for these graces God has given to you.

FRESH-AIR PRAYER

This Exercise may be easier to do in the country or by the sea - but is not impossible in town! Settle yourself in a spot that feels "right".

Help yourself to focus by beginning with this short prayer:

Breathing in gently:	*Breathing out*
Lord, open my mind...	that I may know Your Presence
Open my heart...	that I may feel Your Presence
Open my eyes...	that I may see Your Presence

Make a note - or sketch - of all that you see.
Savour the shapes and the colours and the shades of colours.

You may find that it helps to stop for a while and repeat the "focusing-prayer" -
perhaps ask God to open your ears to the sounds of His presence -
your hands to touch His presence -
and so on...

You may like to move to another spot - and repeat the process.
Once you have a feel for this, you will find that you can do it anywhere!

Fifth Week of Lent

FREEDOM AND NEW LIFE

Year A - The Raising of Lazarus (John 11: 1-45)
Year B - Unless a grain of wheat should die. (John 12: 20-33)
Year C - The Woman taken in Adultery (John 6: 1-11)

MONDAY

Scripture: Daniel 13: 1-9, 15-17, 19-30, 33-62; Psalm 22(23); John 8: 1-11

Jesus said, "Where are they? Has no one condemned you?"
"No one sir," she replied.
"Neither do I condemn you," said Jesus, "Go away and don't sin any more."

This Gospel story lends itself to slow reading - sentence by sentence.
Alternatively, pray it imaginatively - placing yourself in the shoes of the woman, of her accusers and of Jesus.

We have all done things that we would hate the world at large to know about.
We feel shame, embarrassment and pain at the memory.
This can be so strong that it deadens us and holds us back in our spiritual life.

In your own words, talk to Jesus about this.
Try to see the same love and forgiveness Jesus that showed to the woman being shown to you.

Express your sorrow, your determination not to sin in the same way again.

Above all, pray for the grace of feeling your release from this sin.
(Again, you may wish to bring this to private Act of Reconciliation - or make it a deep and sincere part of your prayer in a community's Penitential Liturgy)

SATURDAY

Scripture: Kings 4: 18-20; Psalm 16(17); John 11: 1-45
(Alternative readings for 5th Week of Lent)

Jesus cried in a loud voice, "Lazarus, here! Come out!" The dead man came out, his feet and hands bound with bands of stuff and a cloth round his face. Jesus said to them, "Unbind him, let him go free."

Take time to read this Gospel Story slowly.
Try to place yourself in the shoes of Martha, Mary, the villagers and Lazarus.
They were all facing death in one way or another.
How did Jesus bring each of them back to life?
Was Lazarus afraid of death after this?
What does the Story tell you?

REVIEWING THE JOURNEY SO FAR...

Today, we are on the threshold of Holy Week.
This may be a good day to look back over your Lenten "Retreat in Everyday Life".
What have you learnt about Jesus?
What have you learnt about God's love and forgiveness?
What have you learnt about yourself and your own spiritual life?
What has surprised you? What has been healed - started to be?

End by thanking God for the many blessings and graces that you have received during your life - and especially those given during Lent.

FRESH-AIR PRAYER

Take a walk in the countryside.
Repeat the focusing-prayer you used last week.
Look around you and make a sketch or note of all the things that are dead - or look dead.
Now look again - and find as many signs of the coming of Spring as you can.
Look especially for buds and insects among the places that seemed to be dead.
What do you learn about death and new life?

Holy Week

MONDAY

Scripture: Isaiah 42: 1-7; Psalm 26(27); John 12: 1-11

Mary brought a jar of very costly ointment and with it anointed the feet of Jesus, wiping them with her hair; the house was full of the scent of the ointment.

Extravagant gestures of love are embarrassing - to the onlookers and sometimes to the one on the receiving-end!
Jesus receives Mary's love - the fragrance of which fills the whole house.
What gesture of love would you like to offer to Jesus as His Passion draws near?

In your prayer, build up a picture of yourself and Jesus.
Let yourself go and try to imagine yourself doing as Mary did - or your own gesture of love for Jesus.
Feel His love and acceptance of what you give.
(Do not be sad if you can't manage the "grand gesture" on this occasion - Martha simply waited on Him, Lazarus sat with Him at dinner. They loved Him as deeply as Mary did - but differently)

TUESDAY

Scripture: Isaiah 49: 1-6; Psalm 70(71); John 13: 21-33, 36-38

Jesus said, "Where I am going you cannot follow Me now."

Over recent weeks, you have spent a lot of time getting to know Jesus better and, hopefully, growing to love Him more and desiring to follow Him more closely. Reflect on those words as if He was saying them to you.

In your own words, tell Jesus what such a parting would now mean to you.

WEDNESDAY

Scripture: Isaiah 50: 4-9; Psalm 68(69); Matthew 26: 14-25

Jesus said, "One of you is about to betray Me."

Have you been betrayed by someone you trusted?
How did you feel?
How did Jesus feel?

Speak to Jesus of your love and sympathy as He faces betrayal by someone He trusted.

The Triduum

The best Prayer for these three Days is to enter fully into the Liturgies of each Day.
These Prayers are provided for those who really cannot get to the Liturgies.
They may also deepen the experience for those who can attend.

HOLY THURSDAY

(A practical point: Once we enter the Triduum (the Three Days of Holy Thursday, Good Friday and Holy Saturday), you may well find that the spiritual side of your life feels much more important. You may find it useful to do as much of your preparation for the Easter Holiday as you can today - shopping etc. This will leave only the essentials to do on Saturday.)

Scripture: Exodus 12: 1-8,11-14; Psalm 115(116);
1 Corinthians 11: 23-26; John 13: 1-15

Jesus said, "I have given you an example so that you may copy what I have done for you,"

One of the themes of Holy Thursday is of Jesus' commandment - Love one another as I have loved you.
His love is not love bestowed from great height - but is a love that gets down on its knees and gets on with the jobs that no one else wants to do (often because they think that it's beneath them)
Our love has to be like this. a love that is prepared to get its hands dirty.
How can you love like this?

Tell Jesus of your desire to follow His example of love.
Ask Him to help you to find ways to make that love real.

Evening/Night Prayer

If you can't get to Mass or to the Watching afterwards:

Jesus said, "Stay here and keep watch with Me."
Keep a candlelight vigil for as long as you can.
Simply stay there, being with your Lord as He watches and waits.
Try to let your last waking thought be of Jesus in the Garden

Keep as a day of fasting. You may choose to eat little or no food, or not watch television - or choose another way that marks this day out as different.

If you are not attending the Solemn Liturgy:

Read the Passion according to St John.
Read it slowly with plenty of pauses to let the words sink in.

Read through Isaiah 53 - and reflect on how Jesus proved to be the Suffering Servant.

If you have a cross, you may like to offer a sign of veneration.
This can take several forms:
in Taizé, people light candles around the cross -
some will come and touch the cross or rest their forehead against it
in Catholic tradition, people kiss the foot of the cross as part of the Good Friday Liturgy

(N.B. - Remember: you are using a symbol and a gesture to represent how your soul feels in response to the Sacrifice of Jesus. This is *not* idolatry.)

Today is not a day for many words...
tenderness and sadness for the sufferings of Jesus will say far more...

An open-air Way of the Cross
If you are using "Showing the Way" within a group, you will be invited to follow the new Way of the Cross in the Leader's Pack.
Alternatively, you may choose to find a version of the Stations of the Cross that you like - or simply go for a long walk - preferably up a hill.

Take the book - or an account of Jesus' Passion with you - and, perhaps a candle/tee-light and matches.

As you walk the Stations of the Cross or up your hill - stop from time-to-time to light the candle and to reflect on each Station or incident in the Passion story.

At the top, reflect on the death of Jesus - on the reality of what happened - and what it gave to the world.

As you walk back, think about Mary, Mary Magdalene and John as they retraced their steps.
Reflect on how the experience felt.
How has it deepened your understanding of the Passion of Jesus?

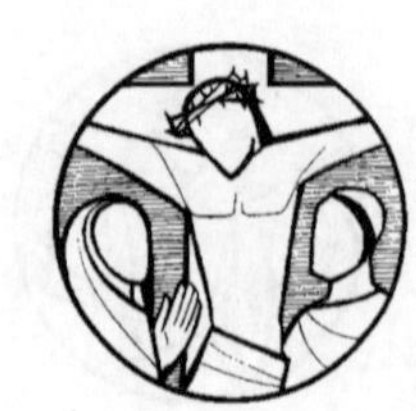

Keep the day as empty as you can - your preparations on Thursday will now prove their worth!

If you are not able to go to a Vigil Service:

At the time when the Vigil is due to start, light a candle and focus your thoughts on what is happening in your parish church: At the time when the Vigil is due to start, (usually around 9 p.m.) switch off the light, light a candle and focus your thoughts on what is happening in churches around the world tonight:

the lighting of the Easter fire - symbolising the triumph of light over darkness

the lighting of the Easter Candle

the Exsultet (found in a Missal or Service Book)

the Readings (selected from the Readings used in the Catholic Liturgy): Genesis 1; Exodus 14: 15 - 15: 1; Romans 6: 3-11; Mark 16: 1-7

"You are looking for Jesus of Nazareth, who was crucified: He is risen, He is not here."

What does it mean to you - that Jesus is alive?
If Jesus is risen, where is He?
Who can you tell? and how?

People are drawn to church on Easter morning - but you may like to begin your celebration earlier in the morning!
Try to go back to the hill where you walked on Good Friday and watch the sun rise. (If you can't manage an early morning visit - try later in the day)
You can go alone - or with a friend - as an Emmaus-type walk.

Try to imagine how it was for the women who went to the tomb…
for Mary Magdalene recognising Jesus in the garden…
for John and Peter arriving to find the grave-cloths but no body…

At the top of the hill, use the scene around you to take in the enormity of what happened that day…

…and what it means today

Jesus is our Risen Lord, the Lord of all Creation…